OUR ETERNAL
INHERITANCE

Applied to Life in this World

SELECTIONS FROM
EPHESIANS 3, 4, 5, 6

GORDON KENWORTHY REED

OUR ETERNAL
INHERITANCE
Applied to Life in this World

SELECTIONS FROM
EPHESIANS 3, 4, 5, 6

BY GORDON KENWORTHY REED

Copyright ©2020 by Tanglewood Publishing

ISBN-13: 978-1-7345087-2-7

All rights reserved.

No part of this book may be reproduced In any from without written permission from Tanglewood Publishing

601-924-5020

www.TanglewoodPublishing.org

fortressbk@aol.com

Book Design and Layout, & Cover Design
by Capsicum Designs
Printed in the United States of America

Contents

A Pastor's Ambition *1*
The Worthy Walk *9*
Building Up The Body *17*
Be Renewed! *25*
Grieving The Holy Spirit..*33*
How To Avoid Satan's Pitfalls..*41*
God's Pattern For Marriage *49*
God's Pattern For Marriage 2: The Role Of The Wife......*57*
God's Pattern For Marriage 3: Parenting God's Way........*65*
God's Armor *75*
The Four "Alls" Of Prayer *85*
A Man Of Grace..*95*

1

A Pastor's Ambition

EPHESIANS 3:14-21

Ambition may be a very good and wholesome thing, or it may become the most destructive power in your life and the lives of all those who know and love you. Self-centered ambition is usually destructive unless it is the kind of ambition described by Jesus when he said, "Blessed are those who hunger and thirst after righteousness, for they shall be filled." And of course, a desire for true righteousness is not really self-centered at all.

Ambition even for other people may also be a power for evil and harm. Look what's happening to organized sports for children. Parents fighting, cursing, even their own children, violence and even an occasional murder are all happening because the parents are ambitious for their kids to win a game, and make their parents proud. The list could go on and on of lives ruined by ungodly ambition. The insane ambition of Adolph Hitler, and before him Napoleon, both of whom plunged Europe into unbelievable suffering and cost the lives of countless millions all over the world.

But what about godly ambition? Is it wrong for parents to want their children to believe in the Lord Jesus Christ and be saved? Of course not! What about our ambitions expressed when we have our children baptized? Is it wrong for a pastor to be ambitious for a congregation? It could be if the ambition is for personal glory or gain. But on the other hand, a lack of godly ambition could be even worse.

Here in this passage of scripture, we discover a pastor praying for his flock and expressing some of the highest and most noble ambitions on behalf of those whom he loves, and these should be your pastor's ambitions for you ... and for the same reason. Of course he wants you to grow, for this would indicate people being brought to the Lord. Of course he wants you to strive for adequate facilities for future generations to continue to serve the Lord, if He delays His coming. But these things are not at the top of a pastor's ambition list for his congregation by any means. His desires for you are expressed in the words of this passage far better than any words I could make up. Listen as the apostle Paul voices his ambition for the church in Ephesus.

I. First, I take these ambitions before the Father who is rich and abundant in mercy and power to work His wonders in your lives.

Prayer is the first line of defense, the most powerful weapon in the arsenal of faith for believers. Prayer that is according to God's will does prevail when it is expressed in faith and confidence that God hears and answers His children when they come to Him. Prayer must also be offered in great humility, knowing that it must be asking what we are not worthy to request from One who is worthy of all our love and commitment. So the Apostle comes before God in this spirit, saying "I bow my knees before the Father."

But at the same time, he comes with great hope and optimism because he knows God is rich, overflowing, and perfectly capable of doing all and more than he can ask or even think.

When you pray, you should always keep in mind that God is infinite, eternal and unchangeable in His power, His mercy, His love, His wisdom; or as we so often express it, "In His being, wisdom, power, holiness, justice, goodness and truth." Confidence in God and these glorious attributes of His character will change your prayer life and indeed will change your life!

II. My request and desire for you is that you might be strengthened through the Holy Spirit, in the inner person so that Christ may dwell in your hearts through faith.

The Holy Spirit is the source of all spiritual strength. We are His temple. He is in all believers, but not all believers are yielded and experience His fullness; hence the prayer. All believers should be constantly praying for His quickening power to be at work in their lives. When that happens, then Christ dwells in you. The Holy Spirit's ministry makes Christ real and ruling in your inner being. The prayer is not that Christ may drop in on you from time to time, nor even that you would on special occasions be aware and open to His presence, but that He might DWELL or ABIDE IN YOU. This speaks of an ongoing and constant experience, and this has but one condition on your part: faith. Please understand that faith is more than merely believing something is true; it is also a surrender to that truth. Now if this is your experience and if this prayer is answered in your life, a wealth of blessings will follow.

III. The next rung in this prayer ladder is that you maybe rooted and grounded in love.

What a perfect mixed metaphor! Rooted and grounded! The first expression is the analogy of a tree, the second that of a house built on a sure foundation. Put them together and you have the picture of a believer's life in relationship to Christ. In fact, Christ used both figures of speech. He called on believers to abide in Him that they might bear fruit. Psalm 1 speaks of a godly person who is like a tree planted by a river, and bearing fruit continuously. The Sermon on the Mount was brought to its stirring and dramatic climax when Jesus told about the enduring safety of the man who built his house upon a rock. Of course, true biblical doctrine is important in laying the foundation for your life in the Lord, but the Apostle points to Love as the soil in which the tree is planted, and the rock upon which the house is built.

When Jesus would restore fallen Peter to that relationship and that place of ministry from which he had so far fallen, He asked Peter a simple question ..."Do you love me?" However, in this prayer the focus is not on our weak and faulty love for Christ, but on His perfect, powerful, and overflowing love for us.

IV. The next step in this prayer is that you may more fully understand the greatness of Christ's love.

His prayer is that being rooted and grounded in Christ's love, you then may go on to comprehend something of the greatness and the surpassing power of that love. This comprehension is more than a limited degree of intellectual understanding, but experiential knowledge, heart knowledge. Really the only way to even begin to comprehend the greatness of His love is to experience it not only in a once for all conversion but in a day by day, ongoing, ever expanding experience. Once more, Paul uses an analogy to explain it. He wanted the believers in Ephesus to know the length, breadth, height, and depth of a love that surpasses knowledge. What is the analogy? I think of two things. The vast, glorious, and splendid temple in which the Jews worshiped before the Romans destroyed it. Beyond that, I think of John's vision of the New Holy City which was so vast and perfect. It was a perfect cube of 1,500 miles. Though the language was figurative, still it pictured something glorious beyond description. So the love of Christ for His church and for each one of His beloved elect and blood-bought children is immense and inexhaustible.

Conclusion

This prayer of Paul for his beloved congregation which I believe your pastor will appropriate for you, my beloved, will never be fully answered in this life, but it is being answered and will ultimately be answered by your life in heaven, in which the love of Christ will be fully understood, and fully experienced without the flaws of present sin which limit our ability. Then you will truly be filled with the fullness of God.

When we gather around the Lord's table to observe the Lord's supper, we are permitted a taste, a sip with our physical senses which enable us to look beyond the symbol to the perfect saving, forgiving, life-claiming love of our blessed Savior.

Am I just praying an idealistic prayer for you? Is there really any hope of fulfillment? At times, all we see and experience is the failure and brokenness of our lives and of the Church of Jesus Christ, and wonder if it will ever be any different. But wait, like all good prayers, this one ends in a confident doxology of praise. Listen! Learn! Love! "Now unto Him who is able to do exceeding abundantly above all that we ask or think, according to the power which works in us, unto Him be glory in the Church and in Christ Jesus unto all generations forever. AMEN."

Questions for Discussion and Reflection

1. How does Paul explain the Holy Spirit's working within us? What does he say our prayer to the Holy Spirit should be?

2. What is the focus of Paul's prayer for us? How does he want us to understand Christ's love?

3. In this chapter, you read that prayer is "the most powerful weapon in the arsenal of faith for believers." What qualities must we strive to bring to our prayer?

4. In his prayer, what did Paul pray the church would have the strength to do? Why would he make such a prayer for God's people?

2

The Worthy Walk

EPHESIANS 4:1-6

One word the Holy Spirit loves in His description of the godly life is "walk." Our call to worship this morning was a quotation from Micah, "Do justly, love mercy, and walk humbly with thy God." But that word goes all the way back to the dawn of creation, when Adam and Eve walked with God in the garden. Later it was said of righteous Enoch, "he walked with God." The biblical description of Noah is summed up in these words: "Noah was a righteous man, blameless in his generation, and Noah walked with God." Then when God began to form a chosen people through whom Messiah would come, He came to Abraham with the call, "walk before me and be blameless."

So, all through the Old Testament, that expression is used to describe godly living. "Blessed is the man who does not walk in the counsel of the ungodly." God promised Israel as a nation, "I will show you the way in which you must walk." Through Isaiah, God invited His people to experience revival when He said, "Come let us walk in the way of the Lord." Amos raised the question, "Can two walk together except they be agreed?" And with these words he challenged Israel to "walk with God."

Naturally, Jesus, and the later the apostolic writers of the New Testament, picked up on this expression and used it over and over again. The parents of John the Baptist were described as people "who walked in all the commandments and ordinances of the Lord, blamelessly."

Of those who turned their backs on Jesus during His earthly ministry, John reported, "From that time, many of His disciples went back and walked with Him no more." So obviously, the Christian life is described as "walking with the Lord, in the light of His word."

Now, as we begin the practical application of the great doctrinal truths the Apostle has been presenting in the first three chapters of Ephesians, we naturally expect him to call upon believers to "walk with God." And what are these great doctrines he has been proclaiming with such joy and persuasiveness? God's gracious and eternal election of His children, salvation by grace through faith, God's intention to ultimately fill us with the fullness of Christ, and God's power to enable those who are enemies by nature to be brought into the one loving family of God.

Strangely enough, Paul did not encourage believers to

feel a sense of smug superiority because of these great doctrines, but exactly the opposite (a lesson we are still learning in the Presbyterian family of churches). On this foundation, he boldly issued his call.

I. The Call To A Worthy Walk

This call sounds very much like that which is found in Romans 12:1, "I beseech you therefore brethren, by the mercies of God, that you present your bodies a living sacrifice, holy acceptable unto God which is your reasonable service." Yes, the figure of speech is different, but the call is the same. Consider the greatness of God's love and mercy, and respond as true believers should. In Romans, the call is to be living offerings to God. Here the call is to live the kind of life that confesses the Lord and demonstrates that faith is real in your life. This is a call to true unity among believers and a life of holiness. As God has said, "Be holy for I am holy."

Here in essence is what he is saying. "In light of the blessings God's incredible grace has brought into your lives, accept the responsibilities of that relationship." God has adopted us as beloved children, so we are to behave in like manner; believing His teachings, trusting His promises, and obeying His will. It is as if Paul is saying, "If you claim to be followers of Christ, and want others to know whose you are, then live like it!"

So, what constitutes a worthy walk? Let's say you have heard the Holy Spirit speaking to you through the Word, and you're ready to obey, and "walk the walk."

What would that look like?

II. The Characteristics Of A "Worthy Walk"

What follows is a concise and compacted description of the Christian life as God intends for us to live it. This is a five-fold description, with each aspect depending on and supporting all the rest.

The first of these is LOWLINESS OR HUMILITY. Having been so unworthy of the least of His mercies, and having received the greatest, the true believer is completely humbled by God's saving love. Does it not humble you to know that God's loving purpose has rested upon you from all eternity? How anyone could allow the truth of God's electing grace to make them proud and self-righteous is beyond me. Humility is the first requirement of entering the kingdom. Someone has said there are three basic essentials of the Christian life: humility, humility, humility. Before you can really receive the mercy of God, you must begin by saying, "I am the lost sinner Jesus came to seek and save." As the Roman centurion said to Jesus, "I am not worthy for you to enter my home, just speak the word, and my servant will be healed." Remember Christ's own self description: "Learn of me for I am meek and lowly of heart."

The next word is MEEKNESS. This is not a synonym for weakness; it is the gentleness of the strong, whose strength is controlled by another. Paul called himself a slave of Christ; can we do less? Meekness is not concerned to assert personal rights nor to proclaim great worth, nor even to out-argue others, but to look upon others as being better than yourself. Be like Abraham who gave to lesser Lot the first choice of the land when it was really his.

The believer who walks worthy of Christ's call is LONGSUFFERING. John Calvin taught that the essence of the Christian life is the willingness to suffer long and without retaliation. I know other believers have their faults and weaknesses, and sometimes treat you worse than unbelievers, but if we are to demonstrate before the world the reality of Christ's presence among us, we must suffer long with each other, for "love suffers long and is kind." What is the opposite of longsuffering? Short fuse! And that describes us so well. This is followed by FORBEARANCE. Literally, the language says, "enduring one another in love." What he means is an inner disposition that expresses itself in an outgoingness, true and tender affection towards each other, and especially towards those you call enemies. Remember what Jesus said, "If you love those who love you, what virtue is that?"

All these are to be bundled up and bound together in LOVE. This love is of course supernatural and far beyond the ability of human nature alone. Only Spirit-filled people can obey this call, but isn't that what we claim to be? Only the congregation committed to these elements of the worthy walk, and deeply repentant if any or all are missing, can ever hope to be what God has called us to be, and for which He sent His Beloved Son into the world.

III. The Consequences Of The Worthy Walk

Here is the high ideal, the goal, and the assured results if Christians heed this call to a worthy walk. When this call is followed, there arises a spiritual oneness in the body of faith which astounds and amazes the watching world. Not only is the spiritual health and happiness of the church at stake, but also the ability to evangelize the lost. What lost sinner could be convinced of God's power to save and heal if a body of believers is not at one and at peace with each other? Furthermore, victory over Satan is impossible without this united front of mutual love and defense. Not long ago, I was watching a film about animal life in Africa. A group of lions was attempting to capture a cape buffalo. So long as the herd stayed together, with their great horns of defense pointed outward, the lions hadn't a chance. It was only when at last they were able to isolate one of these magnificent animals from the herd that they could kill and devour it. Don't let Satan isolate you from God's flock. When you see a brother or sister being isolated, rush to their defense and call upon others to join you.

This sort of unity does not come without conscious effort, so we are exhorted to endeavor to keep this unity in the bond of peace. The word 'endeavor' implies two things: a constant, never-ending effort, and diligent prayer. Unity of the Spirit is only possible when congregations and individuals take seriously the call to prayer, even as those first disciples prayed in the upper room as they waited for the outpouring of the Spirit. And when that outpouring came, they were all together in one accord. They ministered to each other, and they turned the world upside down for Christ.

Finally, we are reminded the fundamental reason for this oneness. There is after all but one body, one Spirit, and one hope; one Lord, one faith and one baptism, and one God and Father of all His people. He is above all, through all and incredibly, in you all.

No wonder we are called to "walk worthy of our calling." So much is at stake!

Questions for Discussion and Reflection

1. What are the doctrines Paul tells us we must apply in order to walk with God?

2. What are the five characteristics of a worthy walk with God? Briefly define each characteristic.

3. Why is spiritual unity with our brothers and sisters in Christ so important? What are the specific qualities of this unity?

4. What evidence of unity in Christ do you see in your own congregation? What do you believe would help your congregation grow stronger in this unity?

3

Building Up The Body

EPHESIANS 4:11-16

Turn on your television or radio, open your morning paper or weekly magazine, everywhere you turn you are inundated with advertisements about how to strengthen and build up your body, and become and remain the picture of youth and health forever and ever. (It all started with Charles Atlas, erstwhile 98 pound weakling who became a he-man and kicked sand in the bully's face.) Buy this machine, or that vitamin, or this mineral supplement and your body will become beautiful, your bald head will sprout hair, your wrinkles will disappear, you will even grow new teeth, and members of the opposite sex will swarm around and fight for your attention and affection.

In spite of the title, that is not what this sermon is all about. What this passage of Scripture is all about is a call to believers who are walking that worthy walk to turn their attention and their efforts towards building up the Body of Christ so that it is unified, and each member is fulfilling its proper function in the whole body, jointly knit together in love.

The exhortations and instructions contained in this short passage of Scripture could truly revitalize and even revolutionize our congregation and any congregation determined to put these principles to the test - far more than building a building, as helpful as that may be.

To add emphasis and to motivate us towards obedience to these things, the Apostle first focuses our attention on the risen and ascended Christ who is the Head of the Church and who gives to His Church all the gifts necessary to make the Church what He wants it to be. Even as Moses received the law directly from God and then gave it to Israel, so Christ received the Spirit and gave Him to His people in order to write God's law in their hearts, through pastors He appointed to teach the truth. On the great day of Pentecost, when the Church was born, Simon Peter said of Christ, "Being therefore exalted to the right hand of God, and having received from the Father the promise of the Holy Spirit, Jesus has poured out this which you see today."

Notice that Paul does not omit the cross and suffering of Christ in speaking of His ascension to power and glory, but links the depths of His suffering with the height of his triumph. Both His exaltation and His humiliation are the foundation upon which the church rests.

Now how is the Body to live up to its high calling and fulfill its purpose as the Body of Christ?

I. The Role Of The Pastors Whom Christ Has Given To The Church

If there is a role in the Church which is misunderstood and even misused it is that of the pastor/teacher. Not only is it misunderstood by the members of the Church, but often even more by the pastors themselves. The everyday duties of the pastor involve a lot of things in the minds of some church members; some good, and some not so good. This may range anywhere from picking up the laundry for someone since you're going near there anyway, to being the messenger of death when there's been an accident (Lee Easterly's classic annual request). The widely held view goes something like this: We pay the pastor to do ministry, and if he lives up to our expectations he will live happily ever after in the manse. (Some call it a parsonage, and when the deacons look at the monthly phone bill they figure he has made too many parson to parson calls). If he doesn't live up to our expectations, there's always a back door and moving van available.

Of course, the pastor contributes to this view of ministry because all too often he simply wants to be the "star of the show." He wants to be the man in charge, and he wants everyone to know it. Unless those of us in the ministry are very careful and constantly guarding ourselves and daily repenting, we will end up more as manager than ministers of Christ.

I will never forget a meeting I had once with a lady who worked at the seminary where I taught for several years. She worked in another building and called and asked for an appointment. When she began to explain why she was there, she broke down into tears. "Pastor," she said, "does God always call men to larger churches and higher salaries? I soon learned what was behind the question. It seemed that the small country church where she was a member had gone through five pastors in seven years. Each time the pastor left for another church, it was always to a larger church with a better salary package. Hence, her question. But what is the biblical model for ministry? Listen and learn, "Christ gave some to be pastor/teacher, for equipping the Saints (that's you) for the work of ministry."

Now that's a unique idea isn't it? The pastor's primary role is to train and equip the members of the Church for ministry! How? By faithfully preaching and teaching the Word of God, but just as importantly and even more so, by modeling ministry in his own life, and by a strong prayer life of intercession for the Church as a body and for each of its members.

II. The Work Of Ministry, Building Up The Body Of Christ

What a dynamic concept! Every church member involved in ministry is not only the biblical ideal, it is the norm. If this concept were understood and accepted, there would be no more going to church just to hear a sermon or lesson, but adequate preparation, wholehearted participation in worship, and true loving fellowship with other believers on the Lord's Day. And during the week, engagement in ministry, whether caring for the sick and elderly, or neighborhood evangelism, or teaching. If you want a good pattern for ministry by all members, read Acts 2:42-47.

But never forget that the effectiveness of positive conscious acts of Christian witness depends largely on the life of the person involved. In other words, if you were to go out on a mission of neighborhood evangelism and call on people whom you have ignored or even mistreated, your efforts to bring them to the Lord or even to the church services would be futile. A great example of the concept of every member being a minister is Barnabas, who was neither an apostle nor even an official in the Church, but just a godly man and a church member who loved the Lord and the Church. He probably thought it was no big deal to sell his property and give proceeds from that sale to the apostles to distribute to those in need. After all, that's what the Lord Jesus taught us to do.

And a grim warning may be seen in the hypocrisy of Ananias and his wife Sapphira who sought glory rather than offering truly sacrificial ministry.

Let me commend many of you who demonstrate your understanding of this and your commitment to it, and urge others who are falling short to accept and rededicate yourselves to Christ's Church, so that together we may build up the Body of Christ. Why? To what end?

III. The Three-Fold Goal Of Every Member Ministry

Unity, knowledge of Christ, Christian maturity ... these are the things we strive for as we work together to edify the Church. This is neither the first nor the last time you will hear the call to true unity in the Body of Christ. Unity among believers is based on the triune nature of God: one God, three persons. Within the Church, there is great diversity, but one body. This unity is a spiritual and very real unity. It does not demand that we all look, talk, or even think alike, but that we are joined together in Christ. When Jesus prayed to the Father the night before He was crucified, He asked that His disciples would experience the kind of unity which would convince the world that the Gospel is true.

This unity not only grows out of the knowledge of Christ, but leads to even more of the same. True knowledge of Christ includes an understanding of the truth revealed in God's Word concerning who Christ is, and what He came to do, and what He taught. But it goes beyond this to include a personal relationship to Him that produces Christ-like living.

So as we grow in this understanding and experience, we mature more and more into the fullness of the image of Christ. This is a process never complete in this world. Even Paul himself testified, late in his life, "Not that I have already attained, or am already perfected, but I press on that I may lay hold of that for which Christ Jesus laid hold of me. Brothers, I do not count myself to attained, but one thing I do, I press on towards the goal."

We all must say of ourselves, "I have not yet attained." But what we must honestly ask ourselves is, can we say, "I press on towards the goal of the high calling in Christ Jesus My Lord"? Or put another way, "Am I the minister Christ has called me to be to help build up His body, the Church?" The next big step and the one most churches overlook is moving out of itself to ministries of mercy, and adding to the kingdom those for whom Christ died. But that's another sermon for another time.

Questions for Discussion and Reflection

1. What is the three-fold goal of "every member ministry"?

2. According to this passage, what is the ultimate goal of "equipping the saints for the work of ministry"?

3. Reflect upon the idea that we are all ministers in the Church. How do you describe your work as a minister among God's people? In what ways might your gifts and abilities lead you toward fuller ministry within your church family?

4. Does your congregation reflect the life described by Paul in this passage? Discuss its strengths and weaknesses. How might the weaknesses be transformed into strengths?

5. How can churches stir up their members to use their gifts toward the building-up of the Body of Christ?

4

Be Renewed!

EPHESIANS 4:17-24

Long ago, there was a woman whom I shall call by a fictitious name, Smith. She was poor, and she was about as lost as a person could possibly be. She was a drunkard and an immoral person. At one point, she abandoned her five children ranging in ages all the way down to four years old, and left them with her oldest child, a severely retarded 18-year-old girl. When we found them in their mountain shack, they were hungry and cold and scared! We fed them, clothed them, and found them a better place to live. Then the mother sobered up and came home. The next Sunday, she came to church with her children. She was a fright! Poorly clad, toothless (though still a young woman), slovenly in personal care, and unbathed; yet she came to church and came back many times.

There came a day when she asked God to forgive her sins, accepted Jesus Christ as her personal Savior and

Lord, and sought membership in the Church. When the day came for her public profession and baptism, it was difficult to believe this was the same person. She was clean, wore a new dress, and even had her hair "done" for the first time in her life. When she cried, there was no dirt on her face for the tears to wash away. In every sense, she was a renewed person. She had put off the old and put on the new, inside and out. She wanted her outward appearance to bear witness to the renewal of her life, brought about by the miracle of the new birth. On that day, I thought her to be one of the most beautiful persons I had ever seen.

In this passage from Ephesians, the theme is renewal, or how to live a renewed life. This renewal touches all aspects and all relationships. It is constant and ongoing, never static. It must be deliberate and vigorous. It is a work of the Holy Spirit, and at the same time a requirement for all believers. This is what transforms our lives, and it is a glorious experience. Renewal simply means to put off the old and put on the new. Though an inner reality, our renewal by the Holy Spirit is increasingly obvious to others.

When believers who have been apathetic and half-hearted hear God's command to be renewed and obey it, the change in our lives should be no less dramatic than Mrs. Smith's. The call to be renewed is a consistent biblical theme. It is both a once and for all call to make a clean break with the past and the sinful way of life, and at the same time it is a call to a daily experience of being constantly renewed all through your life. The first big question that comes to mind is this:

I. Renewed? From What?

The answer to that question begins back in verse 17. "This I say therefore, and testify in the Lord that you no longer walk as the Gentiles walk." In this context, the word "Gentiles" is synonymous with "unbelievers" or "lost sinners." It is alarming but entirely realistic to have to remind Christians to stop acting like unbelievers. What a pity, what a shame that those of us who are the objects of God's eternal, saving love, who have been adopted as His beloved children, saved by the death of Christ, have to be constantly rebuked for living and acting like those who have never known these glorious truths and have never experienced God's gracious forgiveness.

Does it shock you to read these words written to Christians? It shouldn't if you know your own heart. But certainly it should and does shame us to realize how much of the old nature still remains. Just the words are alarming: futility, darkened understanding, ignorance, hardness of heart, callous, sensuality, impurity, greediness, lust, deceits. Yet believers may and do give in to these sinful attitudes and ways. The question was posed to me very recently, "If what the Bible teaches about the Christian life is true, and if we say we believe it, then why is there such little evidence in our daily lives? Why don't we demonstrate these teachings about love, forgiveness, gentleness, and kindness towards each other?" These are good questions, and we ought to ask ourselves these things constantly.

So we have this exhortation to lay aside our former way

of thinking and living, and don't be conformed to the fallen culture in which we must still live. Paul calls the old way of thinking and living "futility" or emptiness. What is it that motivates people in their lives? It is the quest for happiness, fulfillment, and security or peace. In this quest, the way of the world is bound to end in futility because it does not nor cannot give these things. Solomon bears witness to the emptiness and futility of life apart from God in Ecclesiastes. Realistically, this putting off the old nature is difficult and painful. We love to cling to our old selves, and we are so easily self-deceived. We want desperately to hold on to our so-called freedom and independence, refusing to admit this is an illusion that only serves to keep us in bondage.

II. Renewed: The Fundamental Principle Of The Christian Life

Now the Apostle calls on believers to realize this and to understand that there must be a radical and ever increasing change in their thinking and in their manner of living, and a determination to put off the old and be renewed. In a sense, when they accepted Christ and claimed Him as Savior and Lord, they had already put off the old nature, but BASIC conversion must be followed by and expressed in DAILY conversion. Am I saying you can lose your salvation? Of course not! But this text does call us as believers to be renewed and if indeed we are true believers, this process will be an ongoing reality. The tree of salvation bears salvation fruit.   As to the old, natural way of living, of reacting to people and to circumstances, the Apostle cries out,

"NO LONGER!" God is telling us, "ENOUGH OF THAT!" As to the former manner of life ..."LAY ASIDE." "You did not learn Christ so as to continue in your old ways of thinking and acting."

The next big question is:

III. Renewed, To What?

Having been called to put off the old nature and to be renewed in the spirit of our minds, now we are told to put on the new nature, which is created in the likeness of God in true righteousness and holiness. And the putting off and putting on are both taking place simultaneously. What a challenge! What a wonder! As soon as God IMPUTES righteousness to us by giving us Christ's righteousness as a robe to cover all our hideous sin, He begins to IMPART righteousness, and begins the long, slow, but sure process of remaking us after His own likeness. God's call to us is never just do a little bit better. It is never anything less than His ultimate goal for us, which is true righteousness and holiness. Righteousness refers to our relationship to others, and holiness to our relationship with Him.

There are times when I wish God would be satisfied with just a little improvement in me, but then I know that would leave me far short of what God's has planned for His children. And it would leave me totally incapable of close fellowship with the Lord, now and in eternity.

Notice the balance in this call. It is not just a call to

"DON'T" or "THOU SHALL NOT", but also "DO" and "THOU SHALL." "Put off the old," yes, but also "put on the new." These both go together. We must learn to say no to the old nature of sin, and at the same time joyfully say yes to God's call to positive goodness.

John Newton is a wonderful illustration of this. When God saved him, He called him to put aside his sinful, lustful life, and to leave the slave trade. But God also called him to a life of purity and service as a minister of the Gospel. God used his preaching to bring thousands into the kingdom and used his song, "AMAZING GRACE," to reach the hearts of thousands even to this very day. Now this is also God's call to you. Examine yourself humbly and honestly in the light of God's Word. Then hear and heed the call. Deliberately, consistently put off the old nature and put on Jesus Christ.

When a prisoner is released, he no longer wears the tell-tale prison garb, but is given new clothes to wear. When a young man becomes a Marine, he is given a uniform that lets the world know he is one of the few, the proud, the Marines! Just so, we have been told to take off the old garments that define us as fallen people, and put on the new nature that identifies us as Christ's very own.

Questions for Discussion and Reflection

1. Paul says we are to put on the "new self." What is the new self?

Be Renewed!

2. What is one piece of "old life" clothing that you are having a hard time "putting off"?

3. We have learned that renewal must be ongoing, constantly striving to put off the old and put on the new. Reflect upon what you can do in your daily life – both spiritual and practical - to strive toward continuing growth and renewal.

5

Grieving The Holy Spirit

EPHESIANS 4:20-32

A woman came into her pastor's office one day with a tale of grief and pain. Her husband of almost twenty years had told her that he just didn't love her anymore and wanted a divorce. He assured her there was no one else. Though she believed him, he was lying as is almost always the case in this sort of situation. She had dropped out of college to go to work to put him through school and then through graduate school. She had continued to work while his practice was still struggling, had borne him three beautiful children, and managed to become an excellent cook and home maker. She still loved her husband very much even when she found out there was another woman. Because she loved him, she was heartbroken, grieved to the very depths of her being. I have heard this same story many, many times over, only the names change. Similar stories are told by parents of erring, sinning children, who have broken their parents' hearts.

Grieve is a love word, and in the sense the Bible uses it, especially in this passage of Scripture, it is a word which expresses deep sorrow. It is only possible to cause grief to a person who loves you, because the word by definition means, "to cause sorrow to." There are many ways of sinning against the Holy Spirit, and at least one of the sins committed against Him is unforgivable in this world or the next. I want you to understand what it means to grieve the Holy Spirit so you may also understand how dreadful this sin is, the serious consequences to you and others, and how to avoid and overcome this terrible sin. It would be easy to say, "Well, as long as I don't commit the unforgivable sin against the Holy Spirit, I won't worry about grieving Him." That's about the same as saying, "Well if I don't kill my wife, it's okay if I break her heart." Any and all sin against the Holy Spirit is exceedingly serious, with frightful consequences for the erring believer and for the whole Body of Christ.

I. Why Is It Possible For Us To Grieve The Holy Spirit?

In the first place, because He is a person, and like the Father and the Son at the very core of His nature, He is love. When John said, "God is love," he was including the Holy Spirit. God, the Holy Spirit loves you just as much as the Father who sent His only begotten Son to die for you. He loves you just as much as the Lord Jesus who hung and died on Calvary's cross for you.

Apart from Him, salvation is impossible because He alone can regenerate your heart from death into life.

Your regeneration is in one sense much like what happened to young Mary, when the power of the Most High overshadowed her and she was with child of the Holy Spirit. With man this is impossible, but with God, even the miracle of the new birth is possible.

He imparts eternal life and sustains it, and it is by the Holy Spirit that we grow in Christ and will one day be made perfect in holiness, like our Lord Jesus Himself.

He is the author of every Christian virtue and good fruit. So whenever a believer pollutes his soul by any deceitful, vengeful, covetous, or filthy thought, he is grieving the Holy Spirit, who has made each believer His temple. "What, do you not know that your body is the temple of the Holy Spirit, whom you have from God, and you are not your own?"

The Holy Spirit unites us to Christ, and therefore as Paul said in 1 Corinthians 6:15-16, "Do you not know your bodies are members of Christ. Shall I then take the members of Christ and unite them to a harlot? God forbid!"

It is only the Holy Spirit who brings us true joy, assurance of salvation, and who seals us unto the day of redemption. So what happens when we grieve Him? We lose our joy and assurance of salvation and become ineffective and miserable. And we bring disrepute on the Body of Christ, weakening her in her mission and ministry in the world. We then are like salt without saltiness, which is good for nothing, and like a light hidden because of sin.

It will be by the mighty power of the Holy Spirit that our lowly bodies of dust will be reformed and resurrected like the glorious body of Christ, making us fit to live in God's renewed and perfect creation forever. Should we then risk grieving the Holy Spirit? Grieving Him always leads to resisting His convicting work in our hearts, and leaving us open to deliberate and willful sinning, of which the Bible warns us in gravest terms. In short, the Holy Spirit is HOLY, and His work and purpose in you is to make you holy. Any thought, word, action, or habit which detracts from your growing holiness is a terrible grief to the blessed Holy Spirit.

II. The Sins Which Especially Grieve The Holy Spirit

First of all, we grieve Him by ignoring Him. Let me illustrate. A new person comes into our worship and attempts to become part of our fellowship. If we ignore that person, carelessly or deliberately, we cause grief and separation. Often times in a group of people we do this, and even more often we ignore the Holy Spirit, and just go on talking and acting as if He is not there. We also may be guilty of ignoring His commands and His prompting. If the Holy Spirit's prompting might cause us personal inconvenience, or even discomfort, we just pretend we don't hear Him. But when the Holy Spirit drove Jesus into the wilderness to endure forty days of fasting and temptation, the Lord Jesus willingly went.

When Philip was in the midst of an exciting revival in Samaria, where many were being saved and there was great joy, suddenly and without explanation, he was led to go off into the wilderness alone. But on that lonely road also traveled the Ethiopian eunuch who couldn't understand the Bible or find salvation even though he was seeking the Lord. Then, led by the Spirit, Philip drew near and began to explain that it was Jesus Christ who fulfilled the Isaiah passages the eunuch was reading. In the immediate context of this passage from Ephesians which we read together, it becomes very clear that there are several specific sins which grieve the Holy Spirit, and thus rob us of the joy and blessing of His presence. For when we sin deliberately, He diminishes His activity in our hearts until we repent, and thus leaves us in uncertainty and misery. This does not mean that the Holy Spirit removes Himself from true believers, but they deprive themselves of His fellowship and blunt His work in their hearts And what are these sins?

We are told to "put away LYING." This includes not only the practice of being deceitful with each other, but also condemns sham or pretense, which are simply other forms of deceit. ANGER is another specific cited in this passage. This would include giving in to outbursts of sudden anger or the even more deadly malice, resentment, and hatred. Yes there is such a thing as sinless anger, but it is rare and rarely under control. Personal grudges which you allow to grip your heart, even though justified in your own eyes or even the eyes of others, grieve the Spirit. STEALING is also listed among these Spirit-grieving sins. This of course includes all forms of dishonesty in our dealings with others, or with God. Some people who would never steal from another person, think nothing of stealing from God by withholding His tithe. Withholding wages or claiming wages for work half done are other forms of stealing, but all forms grieve the Spirit.

Then of course, there are the sins of the TONGUE. "Let no unwholesome word proceed out of your mouth. Do you know the literal translation? Let no "rotten" word come out of your mouth. This not only means foul language, but anything which does not build up the other person. In fact, the Holy Spirit leads us to speak words which help and build up, even if in form of rebuke which may be needed. James reminds us that an unruly tongue is controlled by hell itself.

Finally, we are told to put away all BITTERNESS and its ugly fruit. It is impossible to cherish resentment and bitterness against another without grieving the blessed and loving Holy Spirit. These and all kindred sins grieve His holy and loving heart. When He is ignored, thwarted, disobeyed, and when there is no response from believers to the preaching of the Word of God, the Holy Spirit is deeply grieved, and the believer loses both his inner peace, and his right and ability to represent Jesus Christ before a lost, broken, and needy world. And hear this, O best beloved: If none of this really grieves your heart and convicts you, and makes you yearn for the return of the Holy Spirit's work in you, then right at this very moment, you are deeply, deeply grieving the Holy Spirit, and opening your heart to Satan's terrible influence and a host of life ruining sins. Please, please for the Lord's sake, and for your own sake, don't let this happen, and don't let this continue.

Questions for Discussion and Reflection

1. How is it possible that we can grieve the Holy Spirit?

2. Bearing in mind that we are a temple for the Holy Spirit, what happens when we grieve Him?

3. What specific sins particularly grieve the Holy Spirit? When we commit these sins, how is our relationship with the Holy Spirit affected?

4. How does the sin of one member of the Body of Christ affect the entire Body?

6

How To Avoid Satan's Pitfalls

EPHESIANS 5:8-21

The great theme of the latter half of Ephesians is spiritual renewal. In this process of renewal (and it is a process, not a one-time event), we will surely face many pitfalls. As we have been reminded in the previous verses, the call of the old nature to fall back into the very sins from which we have been saved is always a lurking danger, even for mature believers. Since we are living in a culture which revels in self-indulgence of every kind, the idea of self-denial is a foreign concept, hated, ridiculed, and rejected. The stubborn, clinging remnant of our fallen nature is filled with all the germs and viruses of the world, and they are a very real threat to our peace, assurance, testimony, and fellowship with the Risen Lord.

Let me use another figure of speech. One of the great dangers facing soldiers in modern warfare is some version of minefields. This really reached horrifying proportions in World War II. Land mines were responsible for a relatively high percentage of all casualties in combat. One of the most dangerous assignments given to any G.I. was to locate a safe path through the minefields for the other men to follow. As you may well imagine, many men lost their lives trying to find and mark a safe pathway. But oh what good feeling for the men who followed the engineers to see those little flags which marked the safe way through the dangerous ground. In these verses, we may follow the pathway marked by God's faithful witness Paul, and avoid the pitfalls which present such danger to the believers and to the Church. That the pitfalls are real and that they are highly dangerous cannot be denied. In fact, one of the surest ways to fall into one of these pitfalls is to ignore this possibility and to say "it will never happen to me." Rather, we should be asking, "Lord, is it I?"

I. The First Flag On The Safe Pathway Is To Walk In The Light, And Live In The Light

Here the Word reminds us that as children of light, it is our duty to keep walking and living in the light. In 1 John 1:5-7, we hear the apostle of love exhorting believers to walk in the light so that they may avoid the dangers of walking in darkness and falling into the sins of darkness. Here in Ephesians 5:8-14, we are told that since we have come out of the darkness of sin and shame into the light of the Lord, we must take great care to walk in that light if we are to avoid the pitfalls of the old nature and the old way of life in which we once lived. Light shows us the dangers inherent in darkness and allows us to avoid those dangers. (Walking into the bedroom of a crying child to drive away the bears and dragons which everyone knows live under children's beds and in their closets and dressers.)

We have been "sons of disobedience" but now "we are children of light," so we are called to be faithful in practice to the principles we have affirmed. The verb tense of "walk" implies continual consistency ... walk and keeping on walking in the light. The surest way for believers to fall into old traps and pitfalls is to be inconsistent in our walk with the Lord. The surest way to avoid these same dangers is to keep on walking in the light: a simple formula, but one which seems to escape a lot of Christians.

Does it ever annoy and worry you believing parents when you can't seem to get across to your children, especially teenage children, that hanging out with people who have no respect for God, parents, or any other authority is the best way to get in serious trouble?

The Apostle then goes on, in a mixed metaphor way, to talk about the "fruit" of light, which is the qualities of heart; goodness, righteousness and truth, which are the exact opposites of the "fruit" of darkness, such as evil, unrighteousness, and hypocrisy. In short, if we are behaving as earth-bound people, how will anyone ever know we are heaven-bound? How would we know it? If, according to verse 10, we try to discern and practice what the will of the Lord is, we will find ourselves walking in God's light, and thus avoiding the dangers of darkness by not participating in the deeds of darkness. By the way, if you are seeking more assurance of your relationship with the Lord and your personal salvation, walking in the light of God's Word and producing the fruit of light is the best way I know.

II. The Next Flag Of Safety Is To Walk In Wisdom v. 15-17

So we have found the first little flag which helps us avoid the minefields. What's next? "Look carefully how you walk, not as unwise but as wise." What is a wise person and what is an unwise person? In the context of what is written here, the wise person is the one who searches out the revealed will of the Lord, and acts upon it. This person not only understands the principles of the godly life, but lives by that understanding, making right decisions and choices which are in harmony with the will of God. The difference between knowledge and wisdom is this: the wise person understands the application of knowledge, and also that knowledge is not an end in itself, but only a means whereby one may know and practice God's will. This person sees and seizes opportunity to serve the Lord and to wisely use the time given, knowing as Jesus knew, "I must work the works of Him who sent Me while it is yet day, for the night cometh, when no man can work."

The unwise person, on the other hand, seems unable or unwilling or both to put into practice the principles of godly living, especially in relationship to other people.

One mark of the unwise is the inability to think in terms of consequences. "If I do this, the result will be thus and so." Or, "If I say this, here is what will be the result." Usually, this sort of person is not only oblivious to cause and effect but cares nothing about it, and has but one aim, to prove "I am right, and you are wrong." Such a person always seeks to justify himself in all he says and does, and is constantly seeking affirmation from others as to the rightness of his position or his actions.

III. The Next Is To Be Filled With The Holy Spirit. v. 18.

Every believer is commanded to be constantly filled with the Holy Spirit. Every believer has the promise of Christ that being His disciple entitles him to claim the promise. The Lord told us that even as a good earthly father delights to give his children good food and care, so much more does our perfect Father in heaven delight to give to us His Holy Spirit.

The immediate context of this verse from Ephesians 5:18 contrasts the world's way of finding peace and contentment with God's way. "Do not be drunk with wine, which is dissipation but be filled with the Spirit" is God's formula. Dissipation consists of giving in to all the old tendencies and sins of the fallen nature. It promises everything good and results in everything evil. But the fullness of the Spirit gives to us all that is good, and nothing that is evil. He enables us to see the pitfalls and convicts us of sin when we fall, even if we are unaware that we have fallen. Sometimes, we interpret self-righteousness to be true righteousness. We mistake zeal for self-justification to be zeal for the Lord. It is truly said that a mean and haughty spirit is the vice of the virtuous. The fullness of the Holy Spirit corrects these "hidden" sins. Not only this, but it is by the indwelling Spirit you are enabled to hear, understand, and apply God's Word to your own inner mind and heart, and in your conduct before others.

Now for the final "flag of safety."

IV. Finally We Are To Walk In Constant Worship And Praise, And In Loving Fellowship With Other Believers In The Body Of Christ. v. 19-21

This may well be the most important "flag of safety." When we practice obedience to the command to be filled with the Spirit, this expresses itself most completely in the gathered Church worshiping the Lord. Never under estimate the power and importance of singing in corporate worship. The categories are often overlooked. Psalms, hymns and spiritual songs are all included as a means of worship and of teaching and admonishing one another. The parallel passage in Colossians 3:16-17 makes the use and the importance of congregational singing stand out even more than this passage. There we are instructed to "Let the word of Christ dwell in you richly in all wisdom, teaching, and admonishing one another in psalms, and hymns, and spiritual songs, singing with grace in your hearts to the Lord."

The two-fold purpose of congregational singing is taught by these words. (1) We are "singing with grace in our hearts to the Lord." We are expressing worship, praise, and thanksgiving to God for Himself and for all His attributes and blessings, and we are (2) instructing and admonishing one another by the same method, singing. The hymns we sing in praise of God must be worthy of and express the glory and majesty of His person, and the wonders of His works. Two examples of many we might cite are "Praise to the Lord, the Almighty, the King of creation," and "Holy, holy, holy." The hymns by which we teach and admonish one another must express biblical truth concerning salvation and the Christian life. Two examples we might mention among the many thousands are "O Master, let me walk with Thee" and "Rescue the perishing." The important thing is to "make melody in your heart to the Lord, and to be sure that we sing the truth of His Word.

As we follow these flags of safety, we will find ourselves obeying the final words of this section which are: "Giving thanks always for all things to God the Father in the name of our Lord Jesus Christ, submitting to each other in the fear of God."

Questions for Discussion and Reflection

1. What is the difference between knowledge and wisdom?

2. What are the four "flags of safety" that help us avoid the pitfalls that we encounter in our walk with God?

3. Discuss the reasons that congregational singing in corporate worship is an important safety flag.

4. Considering this passage in its entirety, reflect upon the following questions.

5. a. Am I living as a child of the light? b. Does my life consist of the fruit of light? c. Do I allow the Spirit to fill me every day? d. What do I need to do to align my life with the teachings in these verses?

7

God's Pattern For Marriage

EPHESIANS 5:21-33

If I were asked what is the most abused, ignored, misunderstood, and misapplied passage of Scripture in all the Bible, without hesitation I would point to this one! In times past, it was used as an excuse for tyranny and abuse, both verbal and physical. In this generation, it is often cited as an example of how out of touch the Bible is with the reality of the human condition, and how it must be re-interpreted in light of modern "understanding" and opinion polls so eagerly worshiped by many people. Radical feminism has pointed to this passage with rage and demanded that everyone should either ignore it or, even better, reject it as outmoded and an example of male chauvinism.

The Church has done a very poor job of proclaiming its truth and demonstrating how it MUST be applied in all ages and generations if the home is to be and remain one of the great foundation pillars on which the Church and the nation rest.

The failure of the Church to properly understand, teach, and live by the principles of this great passage from God's Word has brought much misery and even disgrace upon itself and upon the family units within the Church. In times past, the interpretation of this passage was probably influenced by the culture of the day. The same thing is true even today; the culture thrusts itself on the minds of believers as it always has.

Now I dare say that even at this very moment, there are those of you, even in a congregation which affirms its loyalty to Scripture as the very Word of God, who are more than somewhat apprehensive about how this passage of Scripture will be interpreted and applied. (Some men may be nervous because I might say something which would challenge their iron grip on the family, or even worse, I might say that which would challenge their wives' steel grip on the family and challenge them to start fulfilling their God-assigned role. Some women might be nervous lest I re-enforce an interpretation which would encourage their husbands to become tyrannical taskmasters and assume control of something they have controlled and have no intention of giving up.)

To belay those fears, and to encourage both husbands and wives to hear God speaking His truth into the marriage and family relationships, I will first attempt to remind myself and you of the general context which surrounds this passage, and also to show how consistent this passage is with the whole tenor of Scripture from Genesis 1:1 through Revelation 22:21.

I. The Immediate Context And The Transitional Verse

This entire section of Ephesians is all about renewal. Renewal in the personal lives of believers as an ongoing experience, and renewal within the whole Body of Christ. We are told that the "garments" of the old life before conversion must be laid aside, and the "garments" of our new nature in Christ must be put on. Much of this new clothing must be manifested within the Body of Christ as believers learn how to live at peace and with unity and harmony in the Body.

Paul has just finished exhorting believers to offer to God praise and thanksgiving through the singing of psalms and hymns and spiritual songs, by which they also instruct and correct each other. Then he adds that we are to submit to each other out of reverence for Christ. Mutual submission to one another in the various roles God has given us is the key to healthy reciprocal living, and is one mark of being filled with the Holy Spirit. This submission is rooted in Christ's submission to the Father's will, and in the Church being in submission to Christ. It is understandable that submission is a hated concept in the world, but what is neither understandable nor acceptable is for Christians to rebel against submission to each other out of reverence for Christ. In a fallen world, God has established levels and roles of human authority which must be acknowledged and accepted, both in society as a whole and especially in the Church. But even as a shepherd is in a sense submissive to his sheep, to the point of laying down his life for them, so those who have roles of leadership in their God-given roles, must also understand that leadership does require submission in the sense of "laying down our lives" for God's sheep.

II. The Role Of The Husband In God's Design For Healthy Marriages And Families

This brings us to this God-inspired passage from His Word concerning the roles of husband, wives, and children in the family, which is also the pattern for the Church of Jesus Christ. Remember that the key here is to understand that both husband and wives in their respective roles are to be in submission to Christ.

The footnotes in the Reformation Study Bible on this passage are helpful. They point out that Greek writers had addressed the relationships within the family structure for centuries before Paul wrote this letter. The whole thrust of their writings was to show how the male head of the family was to govern the family with emphasis on how to dominate the members. Paul (and Peter) transformed the question to how husbands and fathers can imitate Christ's love for his Church by caring for and loving unselfishly their wives and children. But make no mistake; the Bible does require the husband to be the spiritual leader and head of his household, including his wife and children and others who may live in that household (Richard Rapp).

In Christ, a man and a woman are equal before God, and their roles are complementary, not competitive.

Husbands and Fathers are required by God to exercise leadership, but that leadership is not absolute; it is under the control of Christ and patterned after His loving leadership of the Church. When that role is surrendered to either wife or children, chaos may well develop. When a husband by deliberate initiative or by weak surrender gives up that role, he is laying a burden upon his wife she should not have to carry, and actually weakens her role as a mother. This also produces confusion and rebellion in the children.

You will notice that Paul goes back and forth between the role of the husband and the role of the wife, but for our purpose I will trace first all that is said about the husband's role before looking at the wife's role. The one dominant theme as to the husband's role is that he love his wife as Christ loves the Church. The admonition to love his wife is repeated four times in this one short section, and each time, the love of the husband for the wife is related to Christ's love for the Church. And all these ways we are to love our wives are verbs of doing, not adjectives of mere sentiment. You will also notice that he never once commands the wife to love her husband in so many words, but we'll get to that later. The husband is to love his wife by giving himself up for her (vv.25-27) in order to assist her in her sanctification and growing relationship to Christ. You may protest that sanctification is a work of God's Holy Spirit, as indeed it is, but He does use the loving leadership of the husband to assist the wife in her spiritual walk.

In what sense is the husband to imitate Christ's giving Himself up for the Church? Christ died to save His people and to create a new humanity by the power of His sacrifice. This the husband cannot do, but he can and must be willing to sacrifice himself for the sake of his wife and family. This sort of loving leadership gives assurance and security to the wife and children. It also serves as an example for them to live unselfishly, too. Two of the most common complaints I hear from wives are these: "He is so selfish" and "He is so mean and hateful." Most women would far rather have an unselfish, sacrificing husband than all the flowers and presents money can buy. Several years ago, I made a similar statement in the church I was serving then. A few weeks later, just after Christmas, one of the men in the congregation came to me and said, "You were right, Pastor. I gave my wife all I could possibly afford to buy her for Christmas, and I waited until she had opened all the presents, then gave her a note telling her I wanted to do everything I could possibly do to make her happy and promised to be gentle, kind, complimentary, and unselfish as long as I live. I wish you could have seen the happy look and the tears of joy as she read that note under the Christmas tree." I can't tell you how wonderful it is to discover someone in the congregation may even listen to the sermon, and act on it!

Next, the husband is instructed to nourish and cherish his wife (vv. 28-30). I believe that involves helping her grow spiritually and learning to be totally safe in his love for her. Failure to do this will not only hinder the wife's spiritual development, it will definitely diminish the husband's relationship to the Lord. According to 1

Peter 3:7, even your prayer life is effected by the way you treat your wife. When Paul said that the husband should love his wife as his own body, he was saying two very important things: (1) She is now one body with her husband, and (2) Paul was applying the words of Jesus in the Sermon on the Mount when He said, "Whatever you wish that others would do to you, do also to them."

Next in vv. 31-32, the husband is required to love his wife above all other earthly relationships, including his parents and former family. She must never be an appendage to the husband and his family, but as a new family unit she is his first and most important relationship. And I shall venture one step beyond these words and tell you both, husband and wife, that your relationship to each other takes precedent even over your love for the children. In fact, one sure way to bless your children and enable them to live more content and complete lives is to let them see you love and serve your wife with tenderness and sincerity and with great affection and joy. Do yourselves and your children a great favor, men: love your wives in the same way Christ loved the Church.

Now I have great and exciting news for you, beloved. I am not going to finish this sermon now, but will take up the role of the wife the next time. And then we will take a closer look at how husbands and wives together serve to follow God's rules for raising children for the Lord, which is by far the most important thing you will ever do in your entire life.

Questions for Discussion and Reflection

1. Mutual submission is grounded in Christ's submission to the Father's will. How did Christ submit to the Father?

2. Earlier chapters addressed the different roles that we each have been given in the Body of Christ. In this chapter, we learn that mutual submission to one another in those God-given roles is vital to the life of the Body of Christ. What do you think it means to submit? What is the hardest thing for you about submitting to someone else?

3. What is one area of your life that would benefit from a more submissive attitude? Reflect upon the difference sacrificial love and respect make in relationships.

4. How did Christ express His love for the Church?

5. What does it mean for the husband to be head over his wife as Christ is over the Church?

8

God's Pattern For Marriage 2: The Role Of The Wife

EPHESIANS 5:21-33

In the process of renewal within the Church, the vital place to begin is renewal within the homes which comprise the Church. Having already looked at the role of the husband in relation to his wife, we now turn to consider the role of the wife in relationship to her husband. But first we need to be reminded of two basic principles which apply to both husband and wife. THE FIRST of these PRINCIPLES is found in verse 21 which introduces the whole discussion of husband-wife relationship. "Submit to each other out of reverence for Christ." By these words, the whole idea of marital relationship is to flow out of our relationship to Christ, as Head over His body, the Church. As the passage develops, two things become obvious. First, our marriages are meant to express acceptance of Christ's authority over our lives in all things. Secondly, Christ is our example of mutual submission in the roles He assigns to husbands and wives. This is true both in the husband's role as head of his family, wife included, and also in the wife's response to her husband's headship.

THE SECOND OF THESE PRINCIPLES: There is also by implication the responsibility and the privilege of mutual agape (Christ-like) love all believers have towards each other. If this kind of love is practiced by both husband and wife, truly they will find their yoke is easy and their burden is light. While it is true that the Apostle directly places the responsibility of love on the husband, we are to interpret this and the wife's response to that love in light of these words from the Gospel of John: "A new commandment I give you that you love one another, even as I have loved you. By this will all men know that you are my disciples if you have love one for the other." So, both husband and wife have the duty of loving each other out of reverence for Christ and obedience to His revealed will. However, it is still true that the husband's role of head places the greater responsibility on Him to demonstrate true, godly, self-sacrificing love towards his wife.

I. The First And Primary Duty Of The Wife Presented In This Passage Is That Of Submission

This of course requires a full understanding of what this means, and then a determination to follow the Lord's command to practice this. If this sounds to you like subservience, get that out of your mind. The submission commanded here is after the same manner in which our Lord Jesus submitted to the Father's will. He was motivated by love, honor, and reverence for His Father. This did not make Him less than God, or other than God, but was an expression of the unity within the Trinity as well as the different roles of each Person within the Trinity.

So when the Apostle tells wives to submit to their husbands, this is no doubt the model he has in mind. Submission in the Lord does not mean the wife is any less important than the husband but is a fellow heir along with her husband. Simon Peter referred to the wife as "the weaker vessel" and that makes many women bristle and work hard to prove they are the physical equals of men. However, calling the wife the weaker vessel as compared with the husband is like saying that a priceless Ming vase is weaker than an ugly old iron pot. Both are true, but being weaker in the sense which Peter used it is not an insult, but is intended as motivation for a husband to cherish and protect his priceless wife, which is one way of being obedient to the command, "Husbands, love your wives as Christ loved the Church."

I hesitate to mention this, but since it is a part of the text as well as the cultural context of that day and this, please note that the command is "Wives submit yourselves to your OWN husbands as unto the Lord." In this way, the sacredness and exclusiveness of the marriage vow is upheld and the need for fidelity underscored. How far should this submission go? Certainly in the ideal situation which is seldom achieved, the love of the husband would be so self-giving, so free of petty tyranny, and such a reflection of Christ's pure love for His Church that the believing wife would eagerly and freely submit to the headship of the husband. But since it seldom is that perfect, the temptation for the wife is to think and say, "Well, since my husband's love for me is so imperfect, I don't have to submit to him." That may sound fair and right to you, especially if you are being re-enforced in this attitude by friends, or even your mother, but this is simply not right. Even as your submission to your husband is far from perfect, so is his loving leadership over you and the whole family. Neither husband nor wife should write themselves an excuse for obedience to these commands of love and obedience.

Once more I cite the example of Christ as the model both for husband and wife. "For the husband is the head of the wife, as also Christ is head of the Church, His body, and is Himself its Savior. Now as the church submits to Christ so also the wives should submit in everything to their husbands." Since we have already looked at that verse from the perspective of the husband's duties in some detail, I will only say here that not only is the headship of the husband taught here and in many other places in Scripture, but the nature of that headship is clearly seen. The stress is not primarily on authority per se, but on how this authority which is God given, should be exercised and to what end. Yes, he has authority but this should never be exercised in an arrogant and domineering manner. But as her head, he recognizes her need for protection and nourishment in the faith. Therefore, His leadership should resemble the sacrificial leadership of Christ for His Church. John Calvin had some very insightful things to say about this in his commentary on Ephesians, but his best commentary was the way he treated his beloved wife, Idelette. His love for his wife resembled very strongly the love of Christ for His Church. He was always thoughtful of every need and tried always to shield her from the hatred heaped on him by his enemies. He also showed her great tenderness, understanding her grief over the death of her first husband, and the need of her children for a father's loving care. The account of Calvin's home life shows a side of this great man that few ever bother to discover, and most have a difficult time believing. For her part, Idelette eagerly and sincerely gave herself to his leadership and authority.

In modern America, the pressure is on the wife to accept no authority from her husband no matter how good and Christ-like he might be towards her. If I understand this passage at all, it teaches that a wife who is not in subjection to her husband is not in subjection to the Lord Jesus. Just as a husband who is not following the example of Christ in his headship is not under subjection to Christ either.

II. How Far Does This Submission Extend?

In Dr. Hendrickson's commentary on verse 24 ("Then just as the church is subject to Christ so also wives should be subject to their husbands in everything"), he remarks: "The submission of the Church to Christ is voluntary, wholehearted, sincere, and enthusiastic." It is a submission prompted not only by conviction that this is what God's Word requires of me, but also out of love for Christ in return for His love for me.

This submission should not be partial, but full and complete. I mean by that the wife should not be selective or when it happens to suit her, or as a bargaining chip for something she desires of him, but "in all things."

Are there any exceptions to this "all things"? Yes, of course. Her submission to him should not include any demands on his part which are contrary to God's revealed will, or that would bring harm and danger upon her or the children. God has established laws and principles for His people by which they are to live, and if the husband violates God's revealed will and requires his wife to do so, too, this would be wrong of him and not required of her.

III. What Does It Mean "Let The Wife See That She Respects Her Husband"?

Here, as always in God's Word, there is great wisdom and clear insight into the make-up of the different genders and their needs. The final word to the wife is vital and important to the ongoing function and the happiness of the family unit. There are special needs of the wife which motivated Paul to speak rather long and eloquently concerning the husband's special love for his wife, as a means of meeting those needs. Now we find that one of the most fundamental needs of a husband is addressed in these final words. "Let the wife see to it that she respects her husband." The translation "respect" is preferred over the KJV, "reverence." Properly speaking, reverence is reserved for God alone, and may even suggest awe, dread, or fear. Between husband and wife, there should be no reason for fear of one towards another. If husbands obey the Word for their part, there would never be any reason for the wife to fear him.

But a man, because of the way God made him, has a basic need for respect, especially from his family. This encourages and challenges him to be the best husband and best father he can possibly be, and it recognizes the created order reflected in Eden. Nothing tears down and discourages a man more than for his own wife to withhold that respect upon which he thrives and functions properly as her protector, her pattern, her security, and her joy. So wives, do yourself and your children a great favor, and demonstrate your commitment to the Lord Jesus by being in proper submission and lavishing on your husband the respect God intends him to have. Try God's way, dear ladies. Unlike your husband, He is always right and every command and precept He gives you is for His glory and for your good.

The role of the wife is not easy. As far as that goes, the role of the husband is not easy either. But if both husband and wife follow God's pattern for marriage, they will discover a fullness in that sacred relationship they never dreamed was really possible, and your home may truly become a colony of heaven on earth and not an outpost of hell.

Questions for Discussion and Reflection

1. Take a few moments to reflect again upon Jesus' submission to the Father's will. It was not subservience. What motivated or defined His submission? How did His submission define His relationship to the Father?

2. Now consider submission within the context of marriage and apply the characteristics of Jesus' submission to the Father to this human relationship. Name some examples of a wife submitting to her husband.

3. Name some examples of how we practice submission to the Lord.

9

God's Pattern For Marriage 3: Parenting God's Way

EPHESIANS 6:1-4

I vaguely remember many years ago in the very early years of ministry attempting to preach on biblical parenting. That was before Elizabeth, our first, was born, and of course before the other four came along, too. I also remember tearing up all my sermon notes on parenting by the time the third one came along.

But God's Word has much to say about the duties and privileges of being parents, and very clear and specific directions on how He expects you to raise your children according to His precepts. Unfortunately in the court of public opinion, yes even within the Church, God's way of parenting has been ruled out of date and out of order in favor of more enlightened insights afforded by modern psychology, John Dewey, Dr Spock, and many,

many other gurus whose advice has been proven to have disastrous consequences both for the family and for society as a whole. Yet in spite of the obvious and catastrophic failures, these vain and ungodly concepts of marriage and the family are still accepted as the only way to raise families, and are most ardently defended.

The precepts and promises within these few short verses contain in abbreviated form far more wisdom than all the books in the library on family living put together, which are not based on God's Word. That God puts a very high priority on believers raising godly children, and children responding in trust and obedience cannot be denied. Very clear guidelines are offered in both the Old and New testaments for families living together under God, and even clearer guidelines on raising children to honor and reverence the Lord. If that were not enough, the Scripture also gives clear warnings as to the disastrous effects of failing to raise children in the nurture and admonition of the Lord, both by direct warnings and by tragic examples of parents who failed in this duty and children who rebelled against God and their parents. What is really shocking is that some of the most prominent people in the Old Testament who were such heroes were also dismal failures as parents, primarily because they failed to discipline their children (Eli, Samuel, David). In this passage of Scripture, there are two basic themes advanced: "Children obey your parents" and "Parents rear them wisely and tenderly." Upon faithful obedience to these two precepts rests the hope of the home and family, and yes the Church and the nation. Let's examine them in the same order in which Scripture gives them.

I. Children Obey Your Parents In The Lord

Though it would seem at first glance that the parents should be addressed first, this is the right order because it is the order God the Holy Spirit chose. The Apostle begins these instructions with a simple command: "Children, obey your parents." That is the primary duty children owe God and their parents, especially during those young years of dependence. I could cite at least a dozen or more specific Scriptures which command that children obey their parents, and many dozen more which teach the same thing.

Whatever else their duty might be, this one is primary and basic. At the same time, it is neither easy nor is the command widely obeyed, especially in our culture. The government constantly intrudes into this circle of authority and order and attempts to claim primary responsibility for the training and discipline of children, and our culture is suffering greatly because of this unwarranted and unbiblical take-over of parental rights and responsibilities.

We must understand that when you depend more and more upon the government for needs within the family, you are also surrendering your right to lead and manage your own household. If the government is going to educate and feed your children, they will demand, and are demanding, the right to tell you how to raise them. I know that with the economic burdens families face today, it becomes more and more difficult for mothers to stay at home with their children. But no one and nothing can ever, ever even remotely replace a mother in the home with her children to provide love, care, and training for them. There is an emotional vacuum in children's lives which is so difficult to fill when the mother is not there to meet those needs. Now some mothers do heroically in managing by God's grace to carry that load and also to some degree help provide the financial needs of the family as well. However, in many cases it is simply a matter of not wanting the daily grind of raising children, and the desire for a more affluent life style. Isn't it?

As to the command itself: It is simple, basic, and straight forward. Children owe their parents obedience, honor, and appreciation. Notice what is added. "in the Lord" and "for this is right."

So, in the context of this whole book, and especially the latter part which deals with renewal within the Church, Paul is making his appeal to children not only on the basis of respect and love for their parents, but primarily out of love and obedience to the Lord Jesus Christ. Thus obedience to parents is even more necessary for Christian children, and it affects their relationship with the Lord Jesus, even as all our relationships within the Church and family affect our relationship with the Lord. When Jesus was a child of 12, He went to temple with Mary and Joseph. You know the story of how He was left behind by mistake, and how that for three days His parents frantically searched for Him before finding Him in the temple. There He was asking and answering questions of the most learned scholars. When Mary rebuked Him, His response was respectful and clear.

"Did you not know that I must be about my Father's business?" Yet, aware as He was of His own special identity as God's only begotten Son, He went with His parents and submitted to their authority, leaving to all children a model and example of obedience and respect. Paul added, "for this is right." It is right because God commands it. It is right because where there is respect and obedience to parents and all those in authority whom God places over us, there is a stable and well-functioning unit, whether family, church, or state. It is right because when you obey your parents, you are obeying God, and that is always the right thing to do, unless they command you to disobey a clear stated command of God.

Next Paul quotes from the fifth of the Ten Commandments, which is "Honor your father and your mother, which is the first commandment with promise that it may be well with you and that you may live long upon the earth." God only included the most basic commands of all He gives us in the Ten Commandments, and this is one of them. It is the command which connects our duty to God and our duty to man in one commandment. He calls it the first commandment with promise. By that he means it is the foremost commandment relating to the family, and that it contains a gracious promise of God's blessing when His order for the family is obeyed by all. This does not mean that all good and obedient children will live a long life, or that those who are evil will always die young. But it is a general principle for individuals and for society as a whole. Undisciplined and disobedient children spell the end for families, churches, and nations. Make no mistake about this. The failure to follow and accept this command has tragic and irreversible consequences for all concerned.

II. Fathers Provoke Not Your Children To Wrath, But Bring Them Up In The Nurture And Admonition Of The Lord

Now we come to the parental side of this passage. Please, all parents listen to God's pattern. Accept His word for the raising of your children. Failure to do this will be the worst sin you will ever commit against your children, or against society as a whole. "Fathers, so not provoke your children to anger, but rear them tenderly in the nurture and admonition of the Lord." (Calvin's translation of this is: "Let them be fondly cherished.") When the expression "fathers" is used, it may also in cases like this be translated "parents", and this advice applies to both fathers and mothers. Still it is clear that God places the primary responsibility of leadership upon the fathers. Also, in most cases mothers are by nature better parents then fathers, and so fathers are more in need of direct instructions than mothers.

The instruction here is not to provoke your children to anger. There are a number of ways we may do this, and I think the first one may be over-protection. There are many "dangers, toils and snares" awaiting our children in this world, and it is so easy to become over-protective in our zeal to be protective. "Yes, dear, you may go swimming, but don't get your feet wet" would be one example of this. The goal of parenting is to teach your children to gradually be less dependent on you and more dependent on God. Of course, we must warn them of the dangers involved in living in this world, but not to the extent we deprive them of all necessary risk-taking. This is a delicate balance, but a needed wisdom.

The next way we could drive our children into moody anger is to show favoritism such as Isaac showed towards Esau, and Rebekah showed towards Jacob. This is a cruel wrong to inflict on children. Another way we err is by words which belittle and shame children. "Oh, you're so dumb, why can't you be smart like your big sister or brother?" Closely akin to this is the desire parents sometimes show to relive their lives or their fancies through their children. This is most often seen when fathers try to become the great athletes they never were by pushing their kids into competitive sports. It's most often seen in mothers when they try to take over their daughter's wedding and make their own fantasies come true.

Of course, neglect is also a sure way to drive your children towards deep anger and resentment. Certainly this seems to have played a decisive role in Absalom's rebellion against David. Another sin of David and so often of ours was an inconsistency of his own behavior, and making allowances for himself in disobeying God's laws. When we are inconsistent either in our own behavior or in enforcing the rules of the home, we confuse and anger our children.

Finally, we may err greatly in the way we discipline our children. While being just and strict, we may become unjust and replace godly discipline with ungodly anger, acts of cruelty, and embittering words. Chastening is needed and even children understand this deep down, though they may protest and wail. Even the Bible says that no chastening at the times seems pleasant, but it is so very important--life and destiny shaping. There is a further word about the necessity of chastening at Hebrews 12:3-11.

The greatest test and responsibility parents have towards the Lord and towards their children is to bring them up in the nurture and admonition OF THE LORD, which means train them to think and act biblically. Which in the end means to bring the heart of the children to the heart of the Savior, for after all, He is the One who said, "Suffer the little children to come unto Me and forbid them not, for of such is the kingdom of heaven."

Questions for Discussion and Reflection

1. Scripture commands that parents be both honored and obeyed. What is the difference between 'honor' and 'obey'?

2. What does Paul tell us are the rewards that come from honoring one's parents?

3. We read that the fifth commandment is the commandment that bridges our duty to God with our duty to man. How does this commandment make that connection?

4. Paul calls the fifth commandment the "commandment with a promise." What is that promise?

10

God's Armor

EPHESIANS 6:13-20

Before getting into the details of the armor which God has provided for us in our battles against Satan, I would like to make one thing very clear. All I know about this armor I have learned from reading reliable commentaries. Contrary to anything else you may hear, I did not serve in the Roman army. Now that those rumors have been laid to rest, let's try to understand what the Lord is teaching us in this passage.

Pardon the overlap, but I do want to remind you briefly of what we learned verses 10-12. (1) We have dire need of this armor because we are not able to withstand the power or cunning of Satan in our own strength. Therefore, we are to find our source of power in the Lord, and in the strength of His might. (2) Even though saved by grace and chosen in Christ from before the foundation of the world, we must avail ourselves of this mighty power and this protecting armor lest we are defeated at every turn by Satan, and become ineffective as warriors in Christ's army. (3) We wrestle not against flesh and blood, but against principalities, against powers, against rulers of the darkness of this age, against armies of wickedness in the spiritual realm. Now we may proceed to understand this description of God's armor, and how to use it in our warfare.

I. Therefore Take Up The Whole Armor Of God That You May Be Able To Withstand In The Evil Day (v.13)

Remember that we described the warfare in which we find ourselves as very similar to hand to hand combat, Christian facing a deadly foe very much as the foot soldier in the front lines. The first thing he must do is repulse the charge of the enemy and stay alive so that he may carry the battle to the foe as he wrestles against the power and cunning of the enemy.

Since this is the nature of the battle we face, we are commanded to arm and equip ourselves so we will not be overwhelmed. This has a sense of immediacy about it because we never know just when or how the Devil or his minions may strike. Paul speaks of the "evil day." I think by this he means in that day when you will be tested severely and unexpectedly. So since we never know when these assaults may come, our preparation must be immediate and continual with no letup.

I have three friends who served in Burma during World War II. They were all members of that famed unit known as Merrill's Marauders. This was a guerrilla band of American raiders who operated behind Japanese lines and inflicted serious damage to the invaders, and greatly hampered their efforts to subdue Burma and cut off supplies to the Chinese armies who were resisting the Japanese invaders. All three of these brave men told me that the most difficult and devastating aspect of this operation was that they could never relax or let their guards down for even a moment. They suffered almost 90% casualties, not only to the bombs and bullets of the cagey Jap warriors, but many of these through disease and even fatal fatigue. When the survivors finally emerged from the jungle and were withdrawn from combat, they were so exhausted and yet so keyed up that they were kept in a barbed wire enclosure for weeks for their own protection and for the protection of other soldiers and/or civilians who might come in contact with them.

I am not suggesting that there is an exact parallel between our spiritual battles and what these brave men faced, but I am suggesting there is a similarity in that we must ever be on guard, and ever equipped to resist, and to attack because our enemy may attack at any time and in any situation. So always be prepared so this passage tells us.

"Standing your ground" does not mean we are simply sitting back waiting for any attack which may come, but as we do battle we are both attacking and defending ourselves and in need of God's armor to succeed. That is the nature of warfare, spiritual or military. As the soldier advances against the enemy, he is subjected to counterattack of the most brutal and determined sort. The apostle who wrote these words experienced just that as he "went into all the world to preach the Gospel to every creature." It was while he was fulfilling his calling from Christ, which came to him at the time of his conversion on the Damascus road, that Paul had to face the power and cunning of Satan. His enemies were Jewish fanatics, Pagan people and practices, Roman power, Christian heresies, false brethren, backsliding believers, well-meaning friends, and maybe above all his own inner struggles as he dealt with the reality of unconquered sin in his own heart.

From what I read in Acts, and in all Paul's writings, he was constantly engaged in spiritual battles of one sort or another. Though he had much success and joy in his ministry, he was never free from fightings and fears, within and without. One may almost hear Paul saying, "This was my experience constantly and the only way I ever won was by following the advice I now pass on to you." All true believers, just like Paul, Peter, Timothy, Titus, and other first century Christians, are on a collision course with the powers of Satan and his host because they are after the same people, but for a different reason. Our quest, like the first century believers, is to reach the lost for Christ and to snatch out of Satan's bondage those whom he now has under his control. Do we really think he will surrender them without a fight?

So we have the command to stand and the spiritual armor we are to put on to assure success in this desperate life and death struggle. I think it is a mistake to assume that Paul was thinking in minute detail about the well-armed Roman soldier. Rather, he was using s general description which he possibly could have remembered from his father's past, who may have earned Roman citizenship by serving well in one of the legions. Whether or not this description fits exactly with what a Roman soldier might have worn is beside the point. The main idea is a well-armed warrior, prepared to attack or defend as the occasion might require. Now to the details.

II. The Belt Of Truth

This is the first piece of the armor mentioned, which brings up the question, "Do you really want to engage such a powerful enemy in ongoing battle?" I think back just after 9-11, when the President addressed congress concerning war against terrorists and vowed to carry the fight to its source, primarily the nations which support terrorist organizations. When he said this, the whole congressional assembly rose to their feet in thunderous applause. But then the actual work of carrying the fight to the enemy began, with a little less enthusiasm, and now so many of those who roared their approval are demanding withdrawal and in effect advocating defeat as a national policy. So just be reminded, if you begin to equip yourself for spiritual warfare, there is no turning back. It is for real and it is earnest. In the Roman army, the belt was essential and important. With it, the soldier buckled his tunic, his limbs set free to fight, and both shield and sword were fastened to it when not in use. In our battle, our belt is the truth, or truthfulness. God's truth is the foundation for all our efforts to defeat Satan. Another way of interpreting the meaning of this belt might be expressed this way, "Take the belt of sincerity."

III. The Breastplate Of Righteousness

The breastplate of righteousness is the next part of God's armor. Even as the Roman breastplate covered the body from neck to thigh, front and back, so this spiritual covering must be employed in our warfare. By this description, it is obvious the Apostle is speaking of living a devout and holy life according to God's Word. This is not the only place in which Paul uses the term breastplate. It is alluded to in Romans and II Corinthians, as well as several places in Ephesians. This means that our profession of faith in Christ must be shown in a devout life of obedience to His Word, kindness, purity, and all the virtues called for in the whole Word of God. Without this protection, we have no defense against Satan's attacks, no assurance of salvation, no peace, nor power, and our testimony will be weak and ineffective.

IV. The Shoes Ready To Advance The Gospel Of Peace

History tells us that one of the reasons for the success of Julius Caesar as a military leader was that he equipped his soldiers with sturdy, thick-soled shoes which enabled his men to march quickly and far. Often times they arrived at the scene of battle long before the enemy was prepared, and so won many victories by surprising the opponent before he was prepared to fight. Believers must be ready and eager to advance against Satan, and to bring the saving Gospel to people far and wide. Sometimes I wonder how many of us would still be employed if we displayed the same lackadaisical attitude to our work as we do towards Christ's command to seek the lost for Him.

V. The Shield Of Faith

So now as we boldly set out to live godly lives and to witness to others, we become targets for Satan. How are we to handle this? First, we take up the shield of faith. The Roman shield was large and thick and covered with leather, and was especially used to repel the enemies' missiles which were dipped in pitch and set fire. The shield blunted the sharp arrows and extinguished the fire. Paul said, "Take the shield of faith." Faith is God given, but it must be exercised and developed by constant use. I believe the primary emphasis here is not on what we call saving faith, but daily trust in God's provision and sovereignty.

VI. The Helmet Of Salvation

The verb we translate 'take' may also mean accept, and this seems to be the better choice here. The Roman soldier accepted the helmet from his officer, and we accept God's free gift of salvation. The assurance of salvation is what protects our minds from despair (one of Satan's favorite weapons). We are saved now, and we shall be saved in all the fullness of that word, and so we labor and so we fight against principalities and powers.

VII. The Sword Of The Spirit

Now fully protected, the warrior takes up the sword and advances upon the enemy. The sword is the weapon the Holy Spirit places in our hands, and it is the Word of God, spoken and written by the prophets and apostles under the inspiration of the Holy Spirit. This sword has supernatural powers far beyond the hand of those who wield it, for "the word of our God stands forever," though the grass withers and the flowers fade. It is a "living sword" sharper than any earth-made blade, and pierces to the very thoughts and intentions of the heart. And how are we to use this sword? By proving we are more knowledgeable than other believers? That we of the reformed faith are right and the lesser breeds wrong? Hardly!

Rather, we see this sharp sword exposing sin and guilt before the holy God. But this sword also cuts through doubts and fears and reveals a Savior who receives sinners, forgives and cleanses. Satan is overcome by this sword alone, and with thanksgiving and praise we accept God's gracious gift, our fear replaced with confidence in grace, and we experience the peace of God. God's armor is there. It is proven effective in overcoming the wiles and assaults of Satan. So put in on and bravely face the enemy. God will grant you victory to His glory and your joy.

Questions for Discussion and Reflection

1. Why is it vitally important that we put on the armor of God?

2. Whose responsibility is it to put on the armor?

3. Who or what is it that we are fighting against?

4. What is the difference between using our own strength and being strong in God's might?

5. List each piece of the armor and describe the purpose of each.

6. What pieces of armor are you strong in? How do you think God may want you to use those strengths? What pieces of your armor need strengthening? What steps might God be leading you in to reinforce them?

11

The Four "Alls" Of Prayer

EPHESIANS 6:14-20

When one looks carefully at the detailed description of God's armor, which He commands the believer to put on, there seems to be a glaring omission at first sight. All our lives as Christians, we have been taught the primacy of prayer and its great importance in our Christian walk. Not only so, but the Scriptures continually exhort us to pray, and in one place we are told to pray without ceasing. There is no mention of prayer as a part of the armor we are commanded to wear. But look at the link we see here between the whole armor of God, and prayer.

The Word of God, which is the sword of the Spirit, is our main offensive weapon in resisting and attacking the forces of spiritual evil which surround us. It is very powerful indeed, especially when it is combined with the word of man directed towards God. In our own strength we cannot prevail against enemies so very powerful. So as we don the armor of God, we put on each piece with prayer and seek His empowerment. What are the four "alls" of prayer we find in this passage?

I. Always Praying

The Apostle immediately and directly ties in the putting on of God's armor with the constant exercise of prayer. As the hymn sings, "Put on the Gospel armor, each piece put on with prayer." Prayer may be compared to the lines of communication with headquarters; it is the invisible but real, powerful, and very necessary link with heaven, and with the God of heaven. Prayer is so much more than merely asking for added blessings, though it is that too. But ideally and scripturally prayer is basically communication with God. This includes praise, supplication, intercession, confession, and all the other elements which go into prayer. But it may also take the form of simply weeping in God's presence, yearning for more holiness, sorrow for sin and failure. Or maybe just smiling and laughing in God's direction for sheer joy and happiness.

Oftentimes as I read God's Word, I find myself praying through the words of Scripture I am reading. Yes, I believe as C.S. Lewis wrote that some prayers are wordless when we are simply overwhelmed with a sense of His nearness and other emotions for which no words are adequate. At such times, the Spirit Himself makes intercession for us with "groanings which cannot be uttered." Obviously, the constant and conscious state of prayer does not require you to bow your head and close your eyes. This could be very dangerous to you and everyone else on a busy street or interstate. But there are many times when praying almost demands that we are on our knees and even on our faces before God if we are physically able. Not that sincere prayer cannot take place in other postures. Martin Luther advocated standing or walking as we pray so that we are not distracted in our minds by other thoughts.

II. All Prayer And Supplication

When the Apostle uses this expression, "Praying with all prayer and supplication in the Spirit," he speaks even more directly to the variety and comprehensiveness of prayer. Though prayer is a very general word which covers not only our frantic cries for help in emergencies, but also confession of sin, asking for cleansing and forgiveness, adoration and thanksgiving, and intercession for others, it also suggests (at least to me) that there should be more specific prayers. By this I mean a general prayer such as "Bless our missionaries on home and foreign fields" should be replaced with names and known needs of those whom we support in this work, and intercession for those they are trying to reach for Christ. It is one thing to pray for "all the missionaries in Mexico and all the people to whom they minister." It is quite another to pray earnestly for the softening of the heart and the conversion of Pedro Gonzales, as requested by missionary Smith in his last e-mail.

This kind of praying is much more demanding. It forces us to take the time and effort to discover needs in the lives of those for whom we are praying. This in turn means we have to demonstrate a genuine concern in the lives of people, and a meaningful involvement so they will tell us their burdens and fears. Our prayers may have more power if we really focus on specific people and situations of need day by day. Maybe if we prayed for one family in our church each day, or even two or three until we have prayed through the church role, we would see more results in our praying, and we will most certainly gain a new sense of closeness to the whole Body.

Notice, too, how the Apostle adds this expression, "in the Spirit." What does this mean? I think it has to do with being in harmony with the Holy Spirit's striving within us and within those for whom we would pray. The Holy Spirit inspired the Word of God, and the Word is our guide as we pray for each other.

It is very instructive to study the prayers of intercession which are recorded in both the Old and New Testaments. There are many psalms which teach us how to pray for God's people. The prayers of Abraham for Sodom and Gomorrah tell us how to intercede for a corrupt culture. His prayers of intercession for those whom he wronged offer light to us in similar situations. Daniel's prayers for God's people in captivity show us how to confess sins, our own and others, and how to claim God's promises for deliverance and for blessing on His Church. The night-long prayers of Christ before selecting certain men for special service in the Kingdom teach us the great and urgent need for prayer before we select people for offices and for other responsibilities in the Church. His High Priestly prayer for His disciples teaches us how to pray for each other, and especially for those in positions of leadership. His own agony in the garden, just before His arrest, trial, and execution, shows us the need for great earnestness and sincerity when we seek for God's will to be done, especially as we face serious illness and death for ourselves and our dearest loved ones. The prayers of Paul for the body of believers in Ephesus as recorded in 1:15-22 and 3:14-21 teach us how to pray for the Church. When you pray for your church, no words which come to our minds could be more powerful than these two master pieces of intercession.

III. Being Watchful To This End With All Perseverance And Supplication

Being watchful may also mean be alert or be aware. Those people who are unconcerned about the world around them are probably going to be very self-centered and weak in their prayer life. Believers simply must be sensitive to our surroundings if they are to be true prayer warriors. That means we have to know what is going on in our families, with our spouses and children, with our neighborhood and our city, our nation and the world. We must inform ourselves about what is happening in our church, our denomination, and in the world mission enterprise of the Church. Even more important, we must know the will of God which grows out of diligent study of His Word. What are the battles facing the church in our generation? What have and are the giants of Christian thought saying? What are the leading opponents of Christianity saying and doing? What are the "signs of the times" Jesus said we must know and interpret? What is God's plan for the Church in the world? How do we appropriate Christ through the sacraments of the Church? What is our responsibility as a congregation to the community in which we minister?

This I believe is what the Apostle had in mind when he said, "Be watchful (alert) in all perseverance and supplication." Does our corporate prayer life reflect this attitude? Does my and your personal prayer life reflect these concerns? Do you get the same feeling I get when I read this passage, that we have barely begun to delve into what prayer is all about?

IV. For All The Saints

Every time I read those words about the risen Christ that "He ever lives to make intercession for them," I am overwhelmed with gratitude and with awe at the enormity of the task our Lord Jesus has taken upon Himself to be our merciful and faithful High Priest. Don't you suppose it must gladden the heart of the Savior to hear us also make intercession for the Saints according to the will of God? We need to get serious about the ministry of intercession for the whole Church of Jesus Christ. I highly recommend the prayer guide called "Operation World" to show us how to pray for God's work around the whole world. I also highly recommend the directory of your own congregation as a prayer guide. When you use this, keep your eyes open and look at and think about each family as you pray.

I know what I am suggesting would require a radical shift in the use of our time, but doesn't this passage seem to suggest that may be exactly what we need to do? A serious ministry of intercession is very demanding, and requires conscious sacrifice on your part. It is even more demanding and also more urgent than deciding to give a significant percentage of your income to the Lord's work. Have you ever thought about tithing your time to the Lord?

As Paul called upon the church in Ephesus to "make supplication for all the saints," he no doubt had in mind the latent divisions within the church between Jewish and Gentile converts. The tension ran high, and the issues were serious, and the danger of a split church was real. So how are we to understand the application? In every congregation there are many differences of opinion and many lingering bad feelings between people for whatever reasons, past or present, and these differences and bad feelings may and often do erupt into confrontation, hurt feelings, and angry retorts. That is exactly the point at which you ought to be praying for each other. When Jacob was returning to Canaan after twenty years, he remembered how angry his brother Esau had been towards him when he fled. He urgently prayed that God would change Esau's heart towards him. In answer, God changed Jacob's heart as well, and there was a sweet reconciliation between the two brothers when they met. So we "pray for all the saints" and not just for a select few.

V. All Prayers Include Praying For Specific Persons And Needs

Paul adds, "and also pray for me." That he would be released from prison? As much as he longed for that release, and for the joyful privilege of once more setting sail for far away shores there to proclaim the good news, that was not his request. Listen to these words from a man who was in chains day and night, possibly facing death at any moment or whim of Nero; who had no privacy ever, but was chained to a guard, who was prevented from doing the work to which he was called, cut off from friends and all comforts. "Pray for me that words may be given to me that I might open my mouth boldly, to make known the mystery of the Gospel, for which I am an ambassador in chains; that I may speak boldly as I ought to speak." I am quite sure that the church in Ephesus prayed for Paul's release, even as the church in Jerusalem prayed for Peter's release when he was put in prison. Be that as it may, Paul's burden was not his release or relief, but for bold faithfulness on his part to understand and speak the Word of God as he might have opportunity. He asks for prayer that God would give him both word and the courage to speak it.

For many people we need not pray that God would give them boldness to speak, they already have that in measure beyond need, but all of us are much in need of prayer to speak the GOSPEL boldly; to use every opportunity and circumstance to witness well for Christ. The Apostle well knew his own weakness and inability to serve God in his own strength, even as I do. Yet he knew his position, though unseen and unknown by human eye or standard, was one of an ambassador not for men, but for God. How fitting that the one who held the highest office possible should ask for prayers for everyone else before his own need. How Christ-like, how humbling for us. What a pattern for all of us to follow. How many of us, if asked to share one special prayer request above all else, would ask for faithfulness to Christ, and boldness to be a faithful ambassador to press home the appeal of our King that people would be reconciled to God? What possible request could be more urgent than this for any and all believers?

So these are the four "alls" of prayer. How are we doing? I seriously and very firmly believe our churches could truly be transformed into an even more powerful witness to the world around us that needs so desperately for believers to learn how to pray Kingdom prayers.

Questions for Discussion and Reflection

1. Many characteristics, qualities, and elements of prayer are listed in this chapter's discussion. Write them down in list form. Study them. How can you begin to insert these practices into your prayer life?

2. What are the four "alls" of prayer?

3. What is intercessory prayer? How is it different from other types of prayer?

4. What does it mean to be watchful? What are the traits of watchful prayer warriors?

12

A Man Of Grace

EPHESIANS 6:21-24

The book of Ephesians is a study in the grace of God. In chapter 1 we discover the foundation of grace, which is God's electing love. In chapter 2 we read of the need of grace and of God's gracious provision, whereby we who were dead in sin have been made alive in Christ, for by grace we have been saved. In chapter 3 we hear of the amazing breadth of grace which includes both Jew and Gentile to become one body under the headship of Christ Jesus, and also hear a prayer for believers to grow in their understanding of the wonder and power of grace. Chapters 4, 5 and 6 teach the application of grace to our daily walk both in our relationship to the Lord and to His body, the Church. We are told grace enables us to put off the old man and put on the new in all our relationships, and especially in marriage and family matters. Also in chapter 6, we are exhorted to don the whole armor of God that we might overcome the many temptations to misuse the gifts of grace.

Therefore, I think it is very fitting that this book on the work of grace in and through us should end with a brief reference to a man who so beautifully exemplified in his life everything that this book teaches about living a God-pleasing life. What an honor to be counted as one of the great Apostle's best friends and most trusted fellow worker for Christ. Though these words about Tychicus are few and our information about him is limited, still from what little we do know, he was indeed a remarkable man and well worth imitating in our Christian walk. I am so blessed for knowing some people like that over the years; people in whom I have seen the reality of Christ-likeness.

There are a few places in the New Testament where his name appears, and always in a favorable light. We read first about him in just a brief mention in the book of Acts. Other than that, we have this reference in Ephesians, another very similar reference in Colossians, and brief mention of him in 2 Timothy 4:12, and Titus 3:12. You may be thinking, why even pause to think about a man whose name only appears a very few times? Well, is your name mentioned anywhere in the Bible? Are you listed among those who joined with Paul in an all-out effort to evangelize the world for Christ? The Holy Spirit is not a name dropper. If He mentions a person's name, it is for a reason and for an example, good or bad. And this one is for good. So let's see what He wants us to know about Tychicus and why.

I. The Role Of Tychicus In The Early Church As Mentioned In The Book Of Acts.

As indicated, he is first referenced in Acts in a short list of men who went with Paul on his journey back to Jerusalem following his third missionary campaign. Apparently, these seven men, delegates from various churches, went with Paul to help protect him, for after all he was carrying the love offerings from the churches in Macedonia and Asia Minor given to relieve the suffering of the persecuted church in Jerusalem. Right away this tells us he was a man to be trusted and possibly a very sturdy lad others would think twice about before causing any trouble. When John Knox was a young man, long before he became the leader of the church in Scotland, he traveled with young George Wishart, the morning star of the Reformation in Scotland, to protect him as he powerfully preached the Gospel. Knox carried a large sword, probably a claymore to defend Wishart. When it became evident that Cardinal Beaton was determined to have Wishart killed for promoting and preaching the doctrines of the Reformation, Wishart persuaded Knox to "Return to your students. One is sufficient for the sacrifice." Reluctantly Knox obeyed, and Wishart was arrested and summarily burned at the stake for preaching God's Word. The rest of that story is beside the point for this sermon, but Knox went on to become a far more powerful influence for God and the true Church than George Wishart could ever have been.

The point being that Tychicus had a similar role in protecting Paul from harm, thus proving himself to be a brave and faithful friend who would later assume a much more important role when Paul was imprisoned in Rome.

II. The Greater Service Of Tychicus As Mentioned In Ephesians And Colossians Timothy And Titus

If all we had was just the mention of his name in Acts, we might well just note it in passing and no more, but these words in Ephesians give us a portrait which is worthy of looking at closely and considering how we may also fit into this picture. Let me sum up what we find in this man of God.

A. Beloved Brother

As he was closing his letter to the church in Ephesus, Paul reassured the Ephesian Christians by telling them he was sending Tychicus to them in person so they might know more of Paul's circumstances, and that he might strengthen their hearts. He called Tychicus, "the beloved brother." What an honorable and enviable title for anyone to bear. We all have many friends and, I trust, are friends to many people. But a "beloved brother (or sister)" is one far beyond the ordinary, and one with whom you could entrust your very life. Such trust and affection is earned in the crucible of life and mutual suffering. Years ago, I held the hand of a dying saint just before his death. He was a ruling elder in the church I was serving during the travail and turmoil of the founding of the PCA. He was a stalwart supporter and defender. As you may imagine, it was a bruising battle, an fierce attacks came from all sides, both physical and spiritual, but George was always there to encourage and pray. Afterwards, the Lord had led me to other fields of labor, but I never forgot nor was I forgotten. One day, years later when I was serving as pastor at First Presbyterian in Macon Georgia, his daughter called to tell me he was dying and if possible wanted to see me before he went home. A little later when I arrived at his home and bedside, he reached out to me with his smile and hand as we talked about the past like two old veterans who had been in combat together. As his strength was so obviously failing, he said something like this: "You have been to me a father, a son, a brother, a pastor, and a friend, and I just wanted to tell you this before I die. Now I've one more favor to ask. Would you conduct my funeral service if it's okay with the pastor of our church?" Next to hearing the Lord Jesus say "well done," no higher words of praise could these unworthy ears of mine ever hear.

Tychicus was Paul's beloved friend. Are you someone's beloved friend they might trust with their broken heart or their very life? Have you such a friend? Are you such a friend? Why would Paul call Tychicus by that term of honor and endearment? Not only had Tychicus traveled with Paul on part of his trip to Rome, but later had ministered to him in the Roman prison. Both these services would suggest considerable sacrifice in time and safety. Paul recognized that the friendship of this young man had been at considerable cost and risk. When a friend gives you gifts, you no doubt appreciate them, but when you discover those gifts involved sacrifice by your friend, they are all the more dear.

B. Trustworthy Messenger

Paul was deeply concerned for this congregation he loved so well, and no doubt troubled that he was unable to personally visit them for their sakes and his. But being a prisoner in Rome, he could not. A letter was helpful, and in God's wisdom and providence a far greater gift than either he or they realized, for it was to become part of God's revelation to all believers. But he longed for the personal touch. Who could he trust to carry his concern and love? Whose heart beat with the same rhythm as his? It would have to be someone who had proven trustworthy. So Tychicus was the man to travel to the churches as Paul's personal ambassador. He had been faithful over a few things, now he could be trusted with a greater role in service to Christ and His Church.

There are many things better said than written. True communication involves inflection of voice, expressions of face, and sincerity of tone. Paul knew he could trust Tychicus to carry these letters to the churches, and to be able to convey his deep concern and love for them. Being a trustworthy man, he would make sure that all Paul wanted them to know about his situation, Tychicus would get across. He also knew that being a fellow and faithful minister, he would bring strength and comfort to the church, even as Paul had done in the past and would do now if he were free to travel. If you think, "What an honor to be chosen as Paul's personal ambassador" and it was; have you forgotten that Christ has chosen you to be His ambassador to someone?

C. Willing Servant

Obviously Paul also knew Tychicus was a humble, willing, and eager servant of Christ. If that meant being a messenger boy for a greater man, so be it. It was no short trip from Rome to Ephesus and Colossae, and there were many dangers and hazards along the way. There would even be people in both those cities who might not receive Tychicus with open arms, and might even resent the language Paul had used in these letters. When the great Apostle had a point to make or a rebuke to offer, he did not beat around the bush. No doubt Tychicus could have been busy making his own way and establishing his own reputation among the churches. But he must have had a true servant heart. So laying aside all personal ambition, he willingly took upon himself the task assigned. He probably had been challenged in his heart when he read these words which had been written to the Philippians: "Let this mind be in you who was also in Christ Jesus..."

D. A Comforting Presence

Have you ever known a person whose presence and demeanor was a comfort and consolation to you? Tychicus was just that kind of man. He had been with the great Apostle during his long wait and then his trial. So he was sent to bring that same consolation and strength to the anxious believers in Ephesus who were troubled and concerned about their beloved friend and former pastor. If God has given you that gift, be quick and ready to use it, for there are so many fellow

Christians who are in need of just that blessing from you.

E. A Living Benediction

Paul's concluding words were: "Peace be to the brothers, and love and faith from God the Father, and the Lord Jesus Christ. Grace be with all those who love our Lord Jesus Christ in sincerity." Peace, love, faith, grace. Blessed words, needed words, and living words when conveyed by a man like Tychicus and maybe a person like you as well.

God's gifts of grace are marvelous as hopefully we have seen in this book of Ephesians. They are to be received by faith, shared in love that His benediction might rest upon His Church. So, take heart and take heed. You have your own heroes of the faith no doubt as your examples of what you will strive to be like in the Kingdom. Add Tychicus to that hall of fame list, and walk in the pathway he demonstrated, and your church will be greatly blessed of the Lord, and the heart of your pastor will be filled with joy and thanksgiving as he mentions you in prayer and as he bears witness to the blessing you are in his life and ministry.

Questions for Discussion and Reflection

1. Tychicus gives us a model example of how to be a faithful brother or sister in Christ. He presents us with many qualities that comprise a faithful and beloved friend. What does it mean to be reliable, honest, and trustworthy?

2. How do you view yourself in terms of the kind of friendship and brotherhood exemplified by Tychicus? Consider your strengths and weaknesses in this regard.

3. Christ has chosen you to be his ambassador to someone. Can you identify who that person might be?

4. We have read of Paul's suffering during this period of his life, and of how he endured it while carrying on his ministry. How do you manage in times of distress? What can you take from Paul's example to help you through difficult times?

www.ingramcontent.com/pod-product-compliance
Lightning Source LLC
Chambersburg PA
CBHW062117080426
42734CB00012B/2898